Tom Cruise

Unleashing the Maverick within Hollywood

Carlos. J. Stones

Table Of Contents

- Developing his signature style: The evolution of Cruise's on-screen charisma, intensity, and physicality.

CHAPTER THREE: Cultural Phenomenon
- Box office domination: Exploring the blockbuster success of films like "Top Gun," "Rain Man," and the "Mission: Impossible" franchise.
- Balancing commercial appeal and critical acclaim: Cruise's strategic choices in film roles and production involvement.
- Impact on popular culture: The Tom Cruise persona and its influence on fashion, catchphrases, and pop references.

CHAPTER FOUR: The Scientology Controversy
- Tom Cruise's association with Scientology: A detailed exploration of his involvement, public declarations, and impact on his public image.

- Media scrutiny and backlash: Analysis of the controversies surrounding his personal life, relationships, and religious beliefs.
- The Cruise effect: How controversies affected his career and public perception.

CHAPTER FIVE: The Philanthropist
- Tom Cruise's humanitarian efforts: His involvement in various charitable organizations and causes.
- Championing social issues: Exploring his dedication to mental health awareness, disaster relief, and veterans' rights.
- Balancing stardom and activism: The challenges and rewards of leveraging fame for positive change.

CHAPTER SIX: Evolution and Legacy
- Adapting to changing times: Cruise's ability to stay relevant in an ever-evolving film industry.

- Impact on the action genre: Examining his influence on the portrayal of action heroes.
- A lasting legacy: Assessing Tom Cruise's enduring status as a Hollywood legend and his contributions to cinema.

EPILOGUE: The Maverick's Journey Continues
- A glimpse into Tom Cruise's future projects and ambitions.
- Personal reflections: Insights from friends, colleagues, and Cruise himself on his remarkable career.
- Tom Cruise's enduring impact on the entertainment industry and his continued influence on aspiring actors.

INTRODUCTION

Tom Cruise - Unleashing the Maverick within Hollywood

In the annals of Hollywood history, there are few names that elicit as much excitement, intrigue, and controversy as that of Tom Cruise. With his striking good looks, electrifying on-screen presence, and unwavering dedication to his craft, Cruise has become a cinematic icon, leaving an indelible mark on the world of entertainment. From his early breakthroughs to his status as one of the highest-grossing actors of all time, Cruise's journey is a testament to passion, resilience, and the pursuit of excellence.

Born Thomas Cruise Mapother IV on July 3, 1962, in Syracuse, New York, Cruise's humble beginnings belie the colossal impact he would have on the film industry. Raised in a working-class environment, he experienced a childhood marked by constant movement and financial challenges. However, within those circumstances, a fire was ignited within him—an unwavering desire to rise above his circumstances and pursue a career that would captivate audiences around the world.

This biography delves into the life and career of Tom Cruise, exploring the intricate tapestry that has shaped him into the enigmatic and magnetic figure we know today. It traces his journey from a determined young boy with dreams of acting to an international superstar with a global following. With each chapter, we embark on a captivating odyssey through the triumphs, controversies, and personal growth that have defined Cruise's life in the limelight.

We begin by peering into the formative years of Cruise's life, examining his early experiences, family background, and the influences that would shape his trajectory. From the challenges of frequent relocations to the support and encouragement of his mother, we witness the seeds of ambition taking root in his heart, driving him towards an unconventional path in pursuit of his dreams.

As Cruise's story unfolds, we delve into the pivotal moments that propelled him from obscurity to the spotlight. We explore his breakthrough roles in films such as "Risky Business" and "Top Gun," which catapulted him to global fame and established him as a leading man capable of captivating audiences with his charisma and intensity. With each success, Cruise further solidified his status as a box office draw, charming audiences with his magnetic on-screen presence and his commitment to pushing the boundaries of his craft.

However, fame and success were not without their challenges. Cruise's personal life became subject to intense scrutiny, as his involvement with Scientology and public declarations of his beliefs thrust him into the spotlight. Controversies and media speculation often threatened to overshadow his career, but Cruise's unwavering dedication to his craft and his ability to captivate audiences allowed him to weather the storm and emerge stronger than ever.

Beyond his status as a movie star, Cruise's philanthropic endeavors and dedication to social causes reveal a man driven not only by artistic pursuits but also by a desire to make a positive impact on the world. His work in promoting mental health awareness, disaster relief, and veterans' rights highlight a compassionate side to the enigmatic figure that has enchanted audiences for decades.

As we journey through Cruise's life and career, we bear witness to his evolution as an actor, a visionary, and a cultural phenomenon. We examine his influence on the action genre, his collaborations with visionary directors, and his enduring legacy in an industry that constantly evolves.

In this biography, we aim to unravel the enigma of Tom Cruise, peering beyond the headlines and the tabloids to understand the man behind the megawatt smile. Through in-depth research, personal reflections, and insights from those who have worked alongside him, we present a comprehensive portrait of a man who has left an indelible mark on the world of entertainment.

Join us as we embark on a thrilling journey into the life of Tom Cruise—a journey filled with triumphs, controversies, and moments of profound introspection. Brace yourself for an exploration of the life of a true Hollywood maverick, as we delve into the captivating story of Tom Cruise: the man, the legend, and the cinematic icon.

CHAPTER ONE

The Making of a Maverick

Early Life and Upbringing: Tom Cruise's Childhood, Family Background, and Early Interests

Tom Cruise, born Thomas Cruise Mapother IV on July 3, 1962, in Syracuse, New York, had a humble and somewhat tumultuous upbringing that would shape his remarkable journey to become one of Hollywood's biggest stars. Cruise's parents, Mary Lee Pfeiffer and Thomas Cruise Mapother III, divorced when he was just 11 years old, leaving a lasting impact on his early life.

Growing up in a working-class environment, Cruise faced numerous challenges, including frequent moves and financial instability. His family relocated several times during his childhood, settling in various cities like Ottawa, Louisville, and Cincinnati. These frequent relocations often disrupted his education, but they also exposed him to different cultures and environments, fueling his curiosity about the world.

Despite the upheavals, Cruise found solace and stability in his mother's unwavering support. Mary Lee Pfeiffer, a special education teacher, played a vital role in fostering Cruise's love for performing. At an early age, he discovered his passion for acting, inspired by his mother's involvement in local theater productions. Cruise participated in school plays and community theater, where he honed his skills and developed a natural talent for captivating audiences.

As a teenager, Cruise faced additional hurdles. He struggled with dyslexia, a learning disorder that made academic pursuits challenging. However, he refused to let his difficulties define him and instead focused on his artistic abilities. This determination and resilience would prove essential in his pursuit of a career in acting.

Cruise's early interests extended beyond the stage. He developed a fascination with sports, particularly wrestling and football, and even aspired to become a professional athlete. However, a knee injury during his high school years derailed those dreams, redirecting his focus towards his true passion: acting.

After graduating from high school in Glen Ridge, New Jersey, Cruise made the bold decision to move to New York City, where he immersed himself in the vibrant theater scene. Eager to learn and improve his craft, he attended acting classes and auditions while working odd jobs to make ends meet.

Cruise's breakthrough came in 1981 when he landed a supporting role in the film "Taps." Although the film garnered mixed reviews, his performance caught the attention of industry professionals, who recognized his potential. This marked the beginning of a rapid ascent to stardom for the young actor.

Tom Cruise's early life and upbringing instilled in him a tenacious work ethic, a passion for storytelling, and an unwavering determination to succeed. Despite facing numerous challenges and setbacks, he used his difficult experiences as fuel for his artistic pursuits. The support of his mother, coupled with his innate talent and relentless drive, propelled him towards a future that would reshape the landscape of Hollywood.

In the subsequent chapters of his life, Tom Cruise would continue to forge his own path, captivating audiences with his magnetic screen presence, intense performances, and unwavering commitment to his craft.

Discovering a Passion for Acting: His First Steps into the World of Theater and Film

In the vast realm of artistic expression, there are rare individuals who possess an innate talent that effortlessly captivates audiences. Tom Cruise, with his magnetic screen presence and undeniable charisma, is undeniably one of those individuals. But how did this Hollywood titan discover his passion for acting and embark on a journey that would forever change his life?

From an early age, Cruise exhibited a curiosity and thirst for performance. Growing up in a family that constantly moved, he found solace in the realm of theater, where he could transport himself into different worlds and become someone else entirely. These formative experiences laid the foundation for his love affair with the stage and, eventually, the silver screen.

Cruise's first foray into the world of acting came during his childhood and adolescence. Encouraged by his mother, Mary Lee Pfeiffer, who was involved in local theater productions, young Tom eagerly participated in school plays and community theater. These early experiences allowed him to explore his creativity, experiment with different characters, and develop a keen understanding of the craft.

As a teenager, Cruise's passion for acting intensified. Although he faced obstacles, such as dyslexia, which made traditional education challenging, he found solace in the world of performing arts. Despite struggling with reading and writing, he discovered that acting provided a means of expression that transcended the limitations he faced in other academic pursuits.

Upon graduating from high school, Cruise made a bold decision that would shape his destiny. He relocated to the vibrant and bustling city of New York, where he immersed himself in the world of theater. Determined to learn from the best, he enrolled in acting classes and workshops, eager to refine his skills and absorb the wisdom of seasoned professionals.

While honing his craft in New York City, Cruise also faced the realities of life as a struggling actor. He took on odd jobs to make ends meet, experiencing the hustle and grind that so many aspiring artists endure. However, his unwavering dedication to his craft never wavered, and his relentless pursuit of excellence propelled him forward.

Cruise's breakthrough in the film industry came in 1981 when he secured a supporting role in the film "Taps." Although his screen time was limited, his talent and screen presence were undeniable. The film provided a glimpse of the star he would soon become and caught the attention of industry insiders who recognized his potential.

Following this initial success, Cruise's career gained momentum with each subsequent role. He demonstrated an uncanny ability to inhabit his characters, infusing them with depth, vulnerability, and an electric energy that captivated audiences. From his breakthrough role in "Risky Business" to his iconic portrayal of Maverick in "Top Gun," Cruise showcased an undeniable star quality that set him apart from his peers.

Throughout his career, Cruise has demonstrated a willingness to take risks and challenge himself artistically. He has collaborated with visionary directors, including Francis Ford Coppola, Tony Scott, and Stanley Kubrick, pushing the boundaries of his abilities and delving into diverse genres and characters. Whether portraying a charismatic secret agent in the "Mission: Impossible" franchise or showcasing his dramatic range in films like "Rain Man" and "Jerry Maguire," Cruise has proven time and again his versatility and dedication to his craft.

Tom Cruise's journey into the world of theater and film is a testament to his unwavering passion for acting. From his early experiences on stage to his transformation into a global superstar, he has embraced the art form with a fervor and commitment that has propelled him to the pinnacle of success. Through perseverance, talent, and an insatiable hunger for growth, Cruise has left an indelible mark on the world of entertainment and continues to captivate audiences with his remarkable performances.

In the following chapters, we delve deeper into the triumphs, challenges, and personal growth that have shaped Tom Cruise's extraordinary career. Join us as we explore the profound impact he has had on the industry and the enduring legacy of a man whose love for acting has touched the hearts of millions.

Overcoming Challenges: Personal Struggles and Setbacks on the Path to Success

The road to success is seldom smooth, and for Tom Cruise, the journey was no exception. Behind the glitz and glamour of his Hollywood career lay a series of personal struggles and setbacks that tested his resilience and determination. From his battles with dyslexia to navigating tumultuous relationships and facing public controversies, Cruise's path to success was marked by challenges that he ultimately overcame with unwavering strength.

One of the most significant hurdles Cruise faced was his struggle with dyslexia, a learning disorder that made traditional education a formidable challenge. Throughout his schooling, he grappled with reading, writing, and comprehension, which often left him feeling frustrated and discouraged. However, rather than allowing dyslexia to define him, Cruise harnessed his determination and resourcefulness to find alternative ways of learning and expressing himself.

Cruise's dyslexia pushed him to develop a strong work ethic and an unwavering commitment to self-improvement. He sought out acting as an outlet for his creativity and found solace in the immersive world of performing arts.

Through sheer perseverance and dedication, he discovered that his dyslexia did not limit his ability to connect with audiences and tell powerful stories on stage and screen.

In addition to his learning challenges, Cruise faced personal struggles in his relationships and personal life. His high-profile marriages to actresses Mimi Rogers, Nicole Kidman, and Katie Holmes were subject to intense media scrutiny, which often took a toll on his emotional well-being. The breakdown of these relationships brought forth immense personal challenges and forced him to confront the complexities of fame, privacy, and the demands of a public persona.

Despite these challenges, Cruise emerged as a resilient and determined individual. He used his personal experiences to fuel his craft, drawing from the depths of his emotions to deliver authentic and powerful performances. The intensity and vulnerability he displayed on screen resonated with audiences worldwide, forging a deep connection and cementing his status as one of the most compelling actors of his generation.

Public controversies and media scrutiny further tested Cruise's resolve. His association with Scientology, a controversial religious movement, thrust him into the spotlight and subjected him to intense scrutiny. His public declarations of his beliefs and his passionate advocacy for the organization sparked debates and divided opinions. Yet, amidst the media firestorm, Cruise remained steadfast in his convictions and continued to focus on his artistic pursuits.

Throughout his career, Cruise demonstrated an extraordinary ability to bounce back from setbacks and channel adversity into personal and professional growth. His determination to overcome challenges fueled his desire to constantly push the boundaries of his craft and take on daring roles that showcased his range and versatility as an actor.

In the face of personal and professional obstacles, Cruise's resilience and unyielding commitment to his dreams remained unwavering. He turned his struggles into strengths, transforming setbacks into stepping stones on his path to success. His ability to persevere and rise above adversity serves as an inspiration to aspiring actors and individuals alike, proving that with resilience, determination, and a steadfast belief in oneself, it is possible to triumph over even the most formidable challenges.

In the following chapters, we delve deeper into the remarkable career and life of Tom Cruise, exploring his triumphs, controversies, and personal growth. Join us as we uncover the profound impact of his resilience and tenacity, and how he emerged from the shadows of adversity to become one of the most enduring and influential figures in the world of entertainment.

CHAPTER TWO

Rising Star

Breakthrough Role: Analysis of His Breakout Performance in "Risky Business" and Its Impact on His Career

In the annals of cinematic history, there are pivotal moments that forever alter the trajectory of an actor's career. For Tom Cruise, one such transformative moment came with his breakout performance in the 1983 film "Risky Business." This coming-of-age comedy-drama not only catapulted Cruise into the spotlight but also showcased his undeniable talent and established him as a rising star in Hollywood.

Directed by Paul Brickman, "Risky Business" tells the story of Joel

Goodson, a high school student who embarks on a wild journey when his parents leave him alone for a weekend. In the film, Cruise embodied the role of Joel with a magnetic presence, infusing the character with a perfect blend of youthful charm, vulnerability, and an undeniable sense of ambition.

Cruise's portrayal of Joel Goodson in "Risky Business" was a revelation. He brought a youthful exuberance and a natural ability to command the screen, captivating audiences with his charisma and ability to convey complex emotions. From the film's opening moments to its unforgettable conclusion, Cruise's performance was a tour de force that showcased his versatility and hinted at the immense talent that would define his future career.

The film's iconic dance sequence, set to Bob Seger's "Old Time Rock and Roll," became an instant cultural touchstone.

Cruise's energetic and uninhibited performance during this scene not only exemplified his physicality and flair for capturing an audience's attention but also solidified his status as a true star in the making. The dance sequence has since become one of the most memorable moments in cinema, forever associated with Cruise's electrifying presence.

"Risky Business" not only served as a showcase for Cruise's talent but also marked a turning point in his career. The film was a critical and commercial success, resonating with audiences and establishing Cruise as a bankable leading man. His ability to convey both vulnerability and confidence endeared him to viewers, while his undeniable charm made him a heartthrob for a generation of moviegoers.

The impact of "Risky Business" on Cruise's career cannot be overstated.

The film opened doors for him, leading to a string of high-profile roles that showcased his range and versatility. It paved the way for his subsequent collaborations with visionary directors and solidified his status as a box office draw. Cruise's breakout performance in "Risky Business" marked the beginning of a trajectory that would see him become one of the most successful and recognizable actors in the world.

Beyond its immediate impact, "Risky Business" also foreshadowed the qualities that would come to define Cruise's career. The film showcased his intensity, his ability to fully immerse himself in a character, and his relentless commitment to his craft. These qualities would become trademarks of his performances in later films, ensuring his continued success and establishing him as one of the most bankable stars in the industry.

In retrospect, the breakout role of Joel Goodson in "Risky Business" was a seminal moment in Tom Cruise's career. It launched him into the stratosphere of Hollywood stardom, setting the stage for an extraordinary journey filled with iconic roles, critical acclaim, and enduring popularity. His performance in this film not only showcased his immense talent but also served as a springboard for the unparalleled success that would follow.

In the following chapters, we delve deeper into the trajectory of Tom Cruise's career, exploring the films that solidified his status as a Hollywood powerhouse and the enduring impact he has had on the industry. Join us as we uncover the remarkable evolution of a true cinematic icon, propelled by his breakout role in "Risky Business" and driven by an unwavering commitment to his craft.

Collaborations with Visionary Directors: Working with Directors like Francis Ford Coppola, Tony Scott, and Stanley Kubrick

Great actors often find their talents elevated when they collaborate with visionary directors who push the boundaries of filmmaking. Tom Cruise's career has been marked by memorable collaborations with some of the industry's most esteemed filmmakers, including Francis Ford Coppola, Tony Scott, and Stanley Kubrick. Through these partnerships, Cruise not only honed his craft but also showcased his versatility and ability to bring complex characters to life on the silver screen.

One of Cruise's earliest collaborations with a renowned director was his role in Francis Ford Coppola's 1983 film "The Outsiders." Adapted from S.E. Hinton's novel, the film featured an ensemble cast of young talents, including Cruise.

Coppola, a master storyteller, guided Cruise in delivering a nuanced performance as Steve Randle, a member of a group of working-class teenagers. While not a leading role, Cruise's portrayal showcased his ability to imbue even supporting characters with depth and authenticity.

Following "The Outsiders," Cruise's collaboration with director Tony Scott would prove to be a defining partnership in his career. Their first project together was the 1986 blockbuster "Top Gun," a film that propelled Cruise to superstar status. Under Scott's direction, Cruise delivered a career-defining performance as Lieutenant Pete "Maverick" Mitchell, a talented Navy fighter pilot. The film's dynamic aerial sequences and Cruise's charismatic portrayal of Maverick solidified his status as an action star and showcased his ability to anchor a high-octane film.

Cruise and Scott reunited for subsequent collaborations, including "Days of Thunder" (1990) and "Enemy of the State" (1998), further establishing their fruitful creative partnership. Their collaborations showcased Cruise's ability to seamlessly blend intense action with compelling character-driven narratives, resulting in box office successes and further cementing his reputation as a leading man.

One of the most notable collaborations in Cruise's career came in 1999 with the release of Stanley Kubrick's final film, "Eyes Wide Shut." Kubrick, a legendary director known for his meticulous attention to detail and psychological exploration, cast Cruise in the lead role of Dr. Bill Harford. The film delved into themes of sexuality, marriage, and existentialism, challenging Cruise to navigate complex emotional terrain. Working with Kubrick allowed Cruise to push his boundaries as an actor and delve into darker and more introspective material.

Cruise's collaborations with visionary directors expanded beyond these notable names, with partnerships with directors such as Steven Spielberg ("Minority Report" and "War of the Worlds"), Cameron Crowe ("Jerry Maguire" and "Vanilla Sky"), and Paul Thomas Anderson ("Magnolia"). Each collaboration brought out different facets of Cruise's talent, allowing him to explore a diverse range of characters and genres.

Through these collaborations, Cruise demonstrated his ability to adapt to the distinct visions of visionary directors. He embraced their guidance, blending his natural charisma and intensity with their unique storytelling styles. These partnerships not only elevated his performances but also showcased his willingness to take risks and tackle challenging roles that expanded his range as an actor.

Tom Cruise's collaborations with visionary directors have played a significant role in shaping his career and solidifying his status as one of Hollywood's most enduring stars. From Coppola's guidance in his early years to the exploration of complex themes under the guidance of Scott and Kubrick, each collaboration has contributed to Cruise's growth as an artist and his ability to captivate audiences with his dynamic performances.

In the following chapters, we delve deeper into Cruise's filmography and explore the lasting impact of his collaborations with visionary directors. Join us as we uncover the diverse range of roles, genres, and creative visions that have defined Cruise's career, shaped his legacy, and established him as a true cinematic icon.

Developing His Signature Style: The Evolution of Cruise's On-Screen Charisma, Intensity, and Physicality

In the realm of Hollywood, certain actors possess a magnetic quality that sets them apart from the rest. Tom Cruise, with his undeniable on-screen charisma, intensity, and physicality, has cultivated a signature style that has become synonymous with his name. Over the course of his illustrious career, Cruise has honed these attributes, shaping his performances and captivating audiences in the process.

Cruise's journey towards developing his signature style began early in his career, as he explored various roles and genres. With each film, he displayed a unique ability to command the screen, exuding a presence that captivated audiences and left a lasting impact. From his breakthrough roles in films like "Risky Business" and "Top Gun" to his later work in movies such as "Mission: Impossible" and "Collateral," Cruise's evolution as an actor was marked by a commitment to pushing boundaries and exploring new facets of his craft.

One of the defining characteristics of Cruise's style is his magnetic on-screen charisma. From the moment he appears on screen, he effortlessly draws the audience's attention, commanding their gaze with his undeniable presence. Whether he's portraying a charming rogue, a determined hero, or a complex anti-hero, Cruise's charisma shines through, creating an immediate connection with viewers. His ability to capture the essence of a character and bring them to life with authenticity is a testament to his natural talent and his dedication to his craft.

Cruise's performances are also characterized by an intensity that is both captivating and electrifying. He possesses a remarkable ability to convey raw emotions, whether it's the fire in his eyes during high-stakes action sequences or the vulnerability he brings to emotionally charged scenes. This intensity infuses his characters with depth and resonates with audiences on a visceral level. It is this intensity that elevates his performances and makes them truly unforgettable.

Physicality is another key element of Cruise's signature style. Throughout his career, he has embraced physically demanding roles and performed many of his own stunts, showcasing his athleticism and dedication to authenticity. From the high-flying aerial maneuvers in "Top Gun" to the death-defying stunts in the "Mission: Impossible" franchise, Cruise's physicality adds an extra layer of excitement and adrenaline to his performances. It is this commitment to pushing his physical limits that has solidified his status as an action star and garnered him praise for his dedication to his craft.

As Cruise's career has progressed, his signature style has continued to evolve. He has sought out collaborations with visionary directors who challenge him to explore new territories and stretch his abilities. These collaborations have allowed him to delve into darker, more complex characters, showcasing a range and versatility that extends beyond the action genre. Cruise's willingness to take risks and embrace diverse roles demonstrates his commitment to growth as an actor and his desire to constantly reinvent himself on screen.

In essence, Tom Cruise's signature style is a combination of on-screen charisma, intensity, and physicality. It is a style that has captivated audiences for decades and set him apart as a true Hollywood icon. His evolution as an actor and his unwavering commitment to his craft have made him one of the most compelling and enduring figures in the industry.

In the following chapters, we delve deeper into the diverse roles and performances that have defined Cruise's career, exploring how his signature style has evolved and the impact it has had on the world of cinema. Join us as we uncover the remarkable journey of an actor who continues to captivate audiences with his unique blend of charm, intensity, and physical prowess.

CHAPTER THREE

Cultural Phenomenon

Box Office Domination: Exploring the Blockbuster Success of Films like "Top Gun," "Rain Man," and the "Mission: Impossible" Franchise

In the realm of box office success, few actors can rival the consistent prowess of Tom Cruise. Throughout his career, Cruise has proven time and again that he possesses the uncanny ability to draw audiences in, leading to the extraordinary success of his films. From the high-flying adrenaline of "Top Gun" to the emotional depth of "Rain Man" and the thrilling escapades of the "Mission: Impossible" franchise, Cruise's films have dominated the box office, solidifying his status as one of the highest-grossing actors of all time.

One of the pivotal moments in Cruise's career came with the release of "Top Gun" in 1986. Directed by Tony Scott, the film became a cultural phenomenon, capturing the hearts of audiences worldwide. Its blend of action, romance, and exhilarating aerial sequences struck a chord with viewers, propelling it to become the highest-grossing film of that year. Cruise's charismatic performance as Maverick, a talented Navy pilot, endeared him to audiences and established him as a bona fide leading man. The film's immense success solidified Cruise's box office appeal and set the stage for his continued dominance in the industry.

Following the triumph of "Top Gun," Cruise showcased his versatility and range in the 1988 film "Rain Man." Directed by Barry Levinson, the film paired Cruise with Dustin Hoffman, who delivered an unforgettable performance as an autistic savant. The film garnered critical acclaim and became a massive box office success, earning over $350 million worldwide. Cruise's portrayal of Charlie Babbitt, a self-centered man on a transformative journey, demonstrated his ability to deliver emotionally resonant performances and expanded his appeal beyond action-packed blockbusters.

In the mid-1990s, Cruise embarked on a new venture that would further solidify his box office domination—the "Mission: Impossible" franchise. The first film, released in 1996 and directed by Brian De Palma, combined thrilling action, espionage, and intricate plots, all anchored by Cruise's magnetic presence. The film's success spawned a highly successful franchise that has become synonymous with Cruise's name. With each installment, from "Mission: Impossible II" to "Mission: Impossible - Fallout," the franchise has consistently achieved box office success, captivating audiences with its high-octane action sequences, intricate storytelling, and Cruise's relentless commitment to performing his own daring stunts.

Beyond these notable films, Cruise's filmography is dotted with numerous blockbusters that have further solidified his box office domination. Films like "Jerry Maguire," "War of the Worlds," "Minority Report," and "The Last Samurai" all contributed to Cruise's status as a reliable box office draw, earning substantial revenues and cementing his appeal across genres.

The extraordinary success of Cruise's films can be attributed to several factors. Firstly, his on-screen charisma and magnetic presence have consistently attracted audiences, drawing them into the worlds he inhabits. Additionally, Cruise's dedication to delivering high-quality performances, often coupled with his willingness to perform his own stunts, creates a sense of authenticity and excitement that resonates with viewers. Audiences are not only drawn to the spectacle but also the undeniable commitment Cruise brings to his craft.

Furthermore, Cruise's ability to select projects that blend commercial appeal with critical acclaim has contributed to his box office success. He has worked with acclaimed directors and chosen roles that challenge him as an actor, showcasing his range and versatility. This strategic approach has allowed him to maintain his box office dominance while earning the respect of peers and critics alike.

In summary, Tom Cruise's films have consistently dominated the box office, establishing him as one of the most successful and bankable actors in the history of cinema. Whether in high-octane action thrillers or emotionally charged dramas, Cruise's films have captured the imaginations of audiences around the world, resulting in phenomenal box office returns. With each new project, Cruise continues to captivate viewers, leaving an indelible mark on the film industry and solidifying his legacy as a true box office heavyweight.

In the following chapters, we delve deeper into the films that have contributed to Cruise's box office domination, exploring their impact, critical reception, and the enduring appeal of a star whose films consistently captivate audiences and shatter records. Join us as we uncover the remarkable success story of an actor whose cinematic journey continues to enthral moviegoers worldwide.

Balancing Commercial Appeal and Critical Acclaim: Cruise's Strategic

Choices in Film Roles and Production Involvement

Achieving a delicate balance between commercial success and critical acclaim is a challenge that many actors face in the film industry. Tom Cruise, with his unwavering dedication to his craft and keen understanding of audience preferences, has demonstrated a remarkable ability to navigate this balance. Throughout his career, Cruise has made strategic choices in selecting film roles and involving himself in the production process, allowing him to create a diverse filmography that appeals to both mass audiences and critics alike.

Cruise's filmography spans a wide range of genres, from action blockbusters to thought-provoking dramas. His strategic approach to film selection is evident in his ability to choose projects that have broad commercial appeal while still offering substance and artistic merit. By doing so, he has maintained his status as a box office draw while earning critical acclaim for his performances.

One notable example of Cruise's ability to strike this balance is his involvement in the "Mission: Impossible" franchise. As both a producer and lead actor, Cruise has played a crucial role in shaping the direction of these films. While the franchise is known for its high-octane action sequences and thrilling stunts, Cruise and the production team have also prioritized strong narratives, intricate plotting, and compelling characters. This dedication to quality storytelling has allowed the "Mission: Impossible" franchise to transcend the typical expectations of an action series, earning critical praise alongside its massive box office success.

Another example of Cruise's strategic choices is his collaboration with esteemed directors who bring a unique artistic vision to their films. By working with visionary filmmakers such as Paul Thomas Anderson ("Magnolia"), Cameron Crowe ("Jerry Maguire"), and Stanley Kubrick ("Eyes Wide Shut"), Cruise has sought out projects that challenge him as an actor and offer opportunities for critical acclaim. These collaborations have resulted in performances that showcase his versatility, depth, and ability to bring complex characters to life. While these films may not always be commercial blockbusters, they have earned Cruise critical acclaim and solidified his reputation as a respected actor.

Cruise's involvement in film production further highlights his strategic approach. By taking on producer roles, he has exerted creative control and ensured that the projects he is involved in maintain a high standard of quality. This level of involvement allows him to shape the films in ways that align with his artistic vision and maximize their potential for both commercial success and critical recognition.

It is worth noting that Cruise's ability to balance commercial appeal and critical acclaim does not solely rely on his role selection and production involvement. His dedication to delivering strong performances, his commitment to performing daring stunts, and his magnetic on-screen presence all contribute to his enduring popularity and success. Audiences are drawn to Cruise not only for the spectacle but also for the authenticity and passion he brings to each role.

Cruise's strategic choices in film roles and production involvement have been instrumental in maintaining his status as one of Hollywood's most bankable and respected actors. By striking a balance between commercial appeal and critical acclaim, he has built a filmography that resonates with audiences of all kinds. His ability to select projects that showcase his talents while offering substance and artistic merit has solidified his reputation as an actor who consistently delivers quality performances.

In the following chapters, we explore the diverse range of roles and films that have exemplified Cruise's strategic choices, delving into the critical and commercial reception of his projects. Join us as we uncover the remarkable career of an actor who has masterfully balanced commercial success and critical acclaim, leaving an indelible mark on the film industry and captivating audiences worldwide.

Impact on Popular Culture: The Tom Cruise Persona and Its Influence on Fashion, Catchphrases, and Pop References

Few actors have left as indelible a mark on popular culture as Tom Cruise. Through his iconic roles, magnetic on-screen presence, and undeniable charisma, Cruise has not only entertained audiences but also shaped the zeitgeist of various eras. His impact extends beyond the silver screen, influencing fashion trends, popular catchphrases, and becoming a frequent subject of pop culture references.

Cruise's distinctive style has had a significant influence on fashion trends over the years. From his aviator sunglasses in "Top Gun" to his impeccably tailored suits in "Jerry Maguire" and the "Mission: Impossible" franchise, Cruise's on-screen wardrobe has often become synonymous with timeless elegance and effortless cool. His fashion choices have sparked emulation and set trends, making him a style icon for many. Cruise's ability to effortlessly blend classic looks with a modern edge has solidified his status as a fashion influencer, inspiring countless individuals to emulate his iconic style.

In addition to his fashion impact, Cruise's performances have spawned memorable catchphrases and lines that have become ingrained in popular culture. Phrases like "Show me the money!" from "Jerry Maguire" and "I feel the need, the need for speed" from "Top Gun" have transcended their respective films, entering the lexicon of everyday conversations. These catchphrases not only showcase Cruise's ability to deliver memorable lines but also serve as cultural touchstones, instantly recognizable and capable of evoking the emotions and memories associated with his iconic characters.

Beyond fashion and catchphrases, Cruise himself has become a frequent subject of pop culture references and parodies. His intense running style, often referred to as "the Cruise run," has been humorously imitated and referenced in various media, becoming a humorous trope in its own right. Additionally, his portrayal of Ethan Hunt in the "Mission: Impossible" franchise has inspired countless spoofs and parodies, emphasizing his status as a cultural phenomenon.

Cruise's impact on popular culture extends to his personal life as well. His relationships, marriages, and public persona have made him a frequent subject of tabloid gossip and media scrutiny. From his high-profile relationships to his involvement with Scientology, Cruise's personal life has been a topic of fascination for fans and the media alike. His public image, defined by his charismatic presence and unwavering dedication to his craft, has cemented his status as one of the most recognizable and influential figures in popular culture.

Moreover, Cruise's philanthropic efforts and advocacy work have also left an indelible impact on popular culture. His involvement in various charitable causes, including mental health awareness and disaster relief, has raised awareness and inspired others to take action. Cruise's dedication to making a positive impact on the world beyond his acting career has solidified his image as a role model and humanitarian, further enhancing his influence on popular culture.

In summary, Tom Cruise's persona and his contributions to film and popular culture have had a profound impact on various aspects of society. His distinctive style, memorable catchphrases, and presence as a subject of references and parodies have permeated popular culture. Additionally, his influence extends beyond the realm of entertainment, with his philanthropy and advocacy work serving as an inspiration to others. Cruise's enduring legacy is that of an actor and cultural figure who has left an indelible mark on fashion, catchphrases, and the collective consciousness of popular culture.

In the following chapters, we delve deeper into the lasting impact of Tom Cruise on popular culture, exploring the ways in which his persona continues to shape and resonate within society. Join us as we uncover the extraordinary influence of a cultural icon and celebrate the enduring legacy of Tom Cruise.

CHAPTER FOUR

The Scientology Controversy

Tom Cruise's Association with Scientology: A Detailed Exploration of His Involvement, Public Declarations, and Impact on His Public Image

Tom Cruise's association with Scientology is a subject that has generated both intrigue and controversy throughout his career. As one of the most prominent and vocal members of the Church of Scientology, Cruise's involvement with the organization has had a significant impact on his public image and the perception of his personal life. To understand the extent of his association with Scientology, it is essential to delve into his involvement, public declarations, and the ensuing discussions surrounding this aspect of his life.

Cruise's connection to Scientology dates back to the early 1990s when he was introduced to the organization by his then-wife, actress Mimi Rogers. He embraced the teachings and practices of Scientology, and over the years, he became one of its most well-known ambassadors. Cruise's involvement in Scientology has included financial contributions, active participation in the organization's events and initiatives, and vocal advocacy for its beliefs and practices.

Throughout his career, Cruise has made public declarations about his affiliation with Scientology, which have garnered significant media attention. He has openly credited Scientology for its positive impact on his life, citing its teachings and practices as instrumental in helping him overcome personal challenges and achieve success. Cruise's public declarations have often been accompanied by passionate endorsements of Scientology's methodologies, including its controversial practices such as "auditing" and its beliefs regarding the nature of the mind and spirituality.

Cruise's association with Scientology has undoubtedly influenced his public image. While his talent and on-screen charisma have made him one of Hollywood's most enduring stars, his affiliation with the organization has been a subject of intense scrutiny and debate. It has sparked discussions about the separation of an actor's personal beliefs from their professional work and raised questions about the influence of Scientology on Cruise's career choices and relationships.

Critics argue that Cruise's association with Scientology has at times overshadowed his acting achievements and led to a perception of him as an advocate for a controversial organization. This association has been a source of contention, with detractors accusing Cruise of promoting a belief system that has been deemed by some as harmful or manipulative. These criticisms have occasionally impacted public opinion of Cruise, leading to debates about the separation of art from the artist and the ethical responsibilities of public figures.

On the other hand, supporters argue that Cruise's involvement with Scientology is a personal matter, and his commitment to the organization should not overshadow his professional accomplishments. They emphasize his dedication to his craft, his philanthropic efforts, and the positive influence he has had on others through his films and advocacy work. They believe that his association with Scientology should not detract from his contributions to the entertainment industry and his charitable endeavors.

It is important to note that discussions surrounding Cruise's association with Scientology are complex and multifaceted. Public perception and opinions on the matter vary greatly, reflecting the diversity of beliefs and values within society. While some may view his involvement as a positive expression of personal spirituality, others may question the validity and impact of the organization itself.

In conclusion, Tom Cruise's association with Scientology has undeniably influenced his public image and sparked discussions about the role of personal beliefs in the lives of public figures. His involvement, public declarations, and the ensuing debates surrounding Scientology have generated both support and criticism. Ultimately, perceptions of

Cruise's association with the organization are subjective and depend on individual beliefs and values. It is through ongoing conversations and dialogue that a deeper understanding of the complexities surrounding this aspect of Cruise's life can be achieved.

In the following chapters, we continue to explore the remarkable career and life of Tom Cruise, focusing on his accomplishments as an actor, philanthropist, and cultural figure. Join us as we delve into the diverse facets of his legacy, celebrating his contributions to the world of entertainment and his enduring impact on popular culture.

Media Scrutiny and Backlash: Analysis of the Controversies Surrounding Tom Cruise's Personal Life, Relationships, and Religious Beliefs

Throughout his career, Tom Cruise has faced a significant amount of media scrutiny and backlash, with controversies surrounding his personal life, relationships, and religious beliefs often making headlines. As one of Hollywood's most recognizable and influential figures, Cruise's every move has been subjected to intense scrutiny, leading to a range of public controversies and debates. To fully understand the impact of these controversies, it is essential to delve into their nature, explore their origins, and analyze their effects on Cruise's public image and career.

One of the most widely discussed controversies involving Cruise was his highly publicized relationships and marriages. The media's attention were intensely subjected to His marriages to actresses Mimi Rogers, Nicole Kidman, and Katie Holmes. The media's fascination with Cruise's personal life, combined with his high-profile status, led to a constant stream of rumors, paparazzi intrusion, and tabloid headlines. The media scrutiny surrounding his relationships often overshadowed his professional accomplishments and resulted in public debates about the boundaries of privacy for public figures.

Another source of controversy has been Cruise's association with the Church of Scientology. His vocal support and advocacy for the organization have generated both interest and criticism. The Church's practices and beliefs have been a subject of intense scrutiny, leading to debates about the legitimacy, impact, and ethics of Scientology. Some critics have expressed concerns about the organization's alleged practices, questioning its influence on Cruise's personal and professional life. These controversies have raised questions about the separation of an actor's personal beliefs from their public persona and have occasionally impacted Cruise's public image.

Cruise's public statements and actions have also sparked controversy, with some instances attracting backlash and public criticism. One such incident occurred during a television interview in 2005 when he expressed strong support for Scientology and engaged in a heated discussion about psychiatry and psychiatric medication. His remarks were met with widespread backlash from mental health organizations, professionals, and the public, who accused him of promoting pseudoscience and downplaying the importance of mental health treatment.

The controversies surrounding Cruise's personal life, relationships, and religious beliefs have undoubtedly impacted his public image and career. While his talent as an actor has solidified his status as one of Hollywood's most bankable stars, the controversies have at times overshadowed his professional achievements and led to public divisions among fans and audiences. Public perception of Cruise has been influenced by these controversies, with opinions varying widely depending on individual perspectives, beliefs, and values.

It is worth noting that media scrutiny and public backlash are inherent risks faced by public figures, especially those who occupy a prominent place in popular culture. The combination of celebrity status, intense media attention, and public curiosity often magnifies controversies and amplifies their impact. The controversies surrounding Cruise's personal life, relationships, and religious beliefs are indicative of the challenges faced by individuals in the public eye and the heightened scrutiny they experience.

In conclusion, Tom Cruise's personal life, relationships, and religious beliefs have been subjects of intense media scrutiny and public controversies throughout his career. The media's fascination with his personal life, combined with his association with Scientology, has generated ongoing discussions and debates. These controversies have influenced public perception and opinions of Cruise, with varying degrees of support and criticism. The impact of these controversies on his career and public image underscores the challenges faced by individuals in the public eye, emphasizing the complex dynamics between celebrity, privacy, and the freedom to express personal beliefs.

In the following chapters, we delve deeper into the remarkable career and legacy of Tom Cruise, focusing on his contributions as an actor, his philanthropy, and the enduring impact he has had on the world of entertainment. Join us as we celebrate the achievements and explore the multifaceted journey of a cultural icon who continues to captivate audiences and leave an indelible mark on popular culture.

The Cruise Effect: How Controversies Affected Tom Cruise's Career and Public Perception

Controversies, as with any public figure, have the potential to impact an individual's career and public perception. Tom Cruise, despite his remarkable success as an actor, has not been immune to the influence of controversies on his professional trajectory and public image. The controversies surrounding Cruise have varied in nature, ranging from personal relationships and religious beliefs to public statements and media scrutiny.

Understanding the effect of these controversies requires an examination of their impact on Cruise's career and the resulting shifts in public perception.

One of the notable ways in which controversies have affected Cruise's career is through the potential impact on box office performance. Public perception plays a crucial role in determining an actor's box office appeal, as audience support and interest are vital for a film's success. Controversies can lead to divided public opinion, affecting audience willingness to support and invest in an actor's projects. While Cruise's films have generally continued to perform well at the box office, it is possible that some controversies have influenced audience perceptions and contributed to fluctuations in his commercial success.

Controversies can also have implications for an actor's professional relationships within the industry. Film productions involve collaboration and partnerships, and controversies can potentially create tensions and affect working dynamics. The fallout from controversies may result in strained relationships or reduced opportunities within the industry. However, Cruise's stature and longstanding success have allowed him to maintain relationships with prominent directors and secure high-profile roles, demonstrating resilience in the face of challenges.

Furthermore, controversies can shape public perception and influence the way an actor is perceived by audiences and the media. Controversies surrounding Cruise's personal life, relationships, and religious beliefs have sparked public debates, generating divided opinions and occasionally impacting his public image. Media narratives can amplify controversies and contribute to the formation of public opinion. The resulting effect may be a division among fans and audiences, with some expressing unwavering support while others may distance themselves due to personal disagreements or concerns.

It is essential to note that controversies can have different effects depending on the individual and the cultural climate in which they occur. The impact of controversies is influenced by various factors, including the nature of the controversy, the response of the public and media, and the individual's handling of the situation. Cruise's charisma, talent, and longstanding success have provided him with a solid foundation to weather controversies, but the lasting impact on his career and public perception remains a subject of ongoing discussion.

Despite the potential negative effects of controversies, it is crucial to recognize that an actor's body of work and artistic contributions play a significant role in shaping their career and public perception. Cruise's talent and dedication to his craft have allowed him to continually deliver captivating performances, resulting in a body of work that spans decades and encompasses a wide range of memorable roles. This sustained success and commitment to his craft have contributed to his enduring popularity and the resilience of his career in the face of controversies.

In conclusion, controversies have had an impact on Tom Cruise's career and public perception, as is the case with any public figure. The effects of controversies are multifaceted, ranging from potential implications for box office performance and professional relationships to the formation of public opinion and division among audiences. Cruise's sustained success and talent as an actor have provided him with a solid foundation to navigate these challenges. Ultimately, his career trajectory and public perception continue to evolve in response to a complex interplay of factors, including controversies, artistic contributions, and audience reception.

In the following chapters, we delve deeper into the remarkable career and legacy of Tom Cruise, exploring his contributions as an actor, philanthropist, and cultural icon. Join us as we celebrate his achievements and reflect on the enduring impact he has made on the world of entertainment and popular culture.

CHAPTER FIVE
The Philanthropist

Tom Cruise's Humanitarian Efforts: His Involvement in Various Charitable Organizations and Causes

Beyond his immense success as an actor, Tom Cruise has demonstrated a deep commitment to humanitarian causes and has actively contributed to various charitable organizations. Throughout his career, Cruise has used his influence and resources to make a positive impact on the world, supporting causes ranging from mental health awareness to disaster relief efforts. His involvement in philanthropic endeavors showcases his dedication to making a difference and highlights the multifaceted nature of his contributions beyond the realm of entertainment.

One of the notable causes that Cruise has supported is mental health awareness. He has been involved in initiatives aimed at reducing the stigma surrounding mental illness and promoting understanding and empathy. Cruise's advocacy for mental health has included raising awareness about the importance of access to quality mental health care and resources. His public discussions and support have helped bring attention to this critical issue, encouraging individuals to seek help and support those in need.

Cruise has also been actively involved in disaster relief efforts. In times of natural disasters and humanitarian crises, he has offered support and contributed resources to assist affected communities. Whether it's providing financial aid or using his platform to raise awareness and rally support, Cruise has consistently demonstrated a willingness to lend a helping hand to those in need.

Additionally, Cruise has supported organizations dedicated to improving the lives of children. He has been involved with initiatives focused on education, healthcare, and overall well-being. Cruise's commitment to children's causes has extended beyond financial contributions, as he has also made personal visits to hospitals and orphanages to spend time with children and offer support.

Moreover, Cruise has been a strong advocate for the arts and the importance of creativity in society. He has made generous donations to arts organizations, including funding for scholarships and programs aimed at nurturing young talents. Cruise recognizes the transformative power of the arts and the positive impact they can have on individuals and communities.

Cruise's involvement in charitable organizations and causes has been significant, but he has also utilized his platform as a public figure to promote awareness and encourage others to get involved. His dedication to philanthropy and his ability to use his fame for the greater good serve as an inspiration to many.

It is important to note that while Cruise's humanitarian efforts have made a difference in various areas, they have also drawn attention to the complexities surrounding the intersection of celebrity, activism, and the role of public figures in effecting change. Celebrity involvement in philanthropy can generate both praise and criticism, with debates arising about the motivations behind such efforts and the potential impact of celebrity endorsements. However, Cruise's ongoing commitment to multiple causes and his dedication to effecting positive change in the world suggest a genuine desire to make a difference and utilize his platform responsibly.

In summary, Tom Cruise's involvement in charitable organizations and causes underscores his commitment to making a positive impact on the world beyond his successful acting career. His support for mental health awareness, disaster relief efforts, children's causes, and the arts showcases a multifaceted approach to philanthropy. Cruise's dedication to humanitarian efforts serves as an inspiration and highlights the potential for public figures to use their influence and resources for the betterment of society.

In the following chapters, we continue to explore the remarkable career and life of Tom Cruise, focusing on his contributions as an actor, his philanthropy, and the enduring impact he has had on the world of entertainment. Join us as we celebrate the achievements and reflect on the multifaceted journey of a cultural icon who continues to captivate audiences and leave an indelible mark on popular culture.

Championing Social Issues: Exploring Tom Cruise's Dedication to Mental Health Awareness, Disaster Relief, and Veterans' Rights

Tom Cruise, beyond his illustrious acting career, has emerged as a dedicated advocate for various social issues, using his platform and influence to raise awareness and effect positive change. His commitment to causes such as mental health awareness, disaster relief, and veterans' rights showcases his unwavering dedication to making a difference in the lives of others. Cruise's involvement in these areas has helped shine a spotlight on important social issues and has inspired many to take action.

One of the significant social issues that Cruise has championed is mental health awareness. He has been vocal about the importance of understanding and addressing mental health challenges, aiming to reduce the stigma associated with mental illness. Cruise's advocacy includes promoting access to mental health care, encouraging open dialogue, and raising funds for organizations dedicated to research and support. By using his platform to discuss mental health, he has helped bring this critical issue to the forefront and has inspired individuals to seek help and support.

In times of natural disasters and humanitarian crises, Cruise has consistently shown his commitment to disaster relief efforts. His involvement in providing aid and resources to affected communities has been impactful. Whether it's contributing financial support, organizing fundraising events, or actively participating in relief efforts, Cruise has demonstrated a hands-on approach to making a positive impact during times of great need. His involvement has not only provided much-needed assistance to those affected by disasters but has also raised awareness about the importance of ongoing support and rebuilding efforts.

Cruise has also been dedicated to supporting veterans' rights and honoring their sacrifices. He has actively participated in initiatives and organizations that aim to improve the lives of veterans, including advocating for improved healthcare services and mental health support for those who have served in the military. His commitment to veterans' rights has been demonstrated through his involvement in events, fundraising campaigns, and public awareness campaigns. By shining a light on the challenges faced by veterans and advocating for their well-being, Cruise has helped foster a greater sense of appreciation and support for those who have served their countries.

It is worth noting that Cruise's dedication to these social issues extends beyond mere financial contributions or endorsements. His involvement is often hands-on and deeply personal, reflecting his genuine passion for effecting change and making a positive impact on individuals and communities. Cruise's dedication to these causes is a testament to his belief in the power of collective action and the ability to make a difference, regardless of one's professional accomplishments.

By championing mental health awareness, disaster relief, and veterans' rights, Tom Cruise has utilized his influence and resources to bring attention to important social issues. His dedication has not only raised awareness but has also inspired others to get involved and make a difference. Cruise's efforts highlight the potential for individuals in the public eye to leverage their platform for positive change, serving as a role model for activism and social responsibility.

It is important to recognize that addressing complex social issues requires a multifaceted approach and sustained effort from multiple individuals and organizations. While Cruise's contributions have been impactful, they are part of a larger collective effort to effect change and improve the lives of others. His dedication serves as an inspiration for others to take action and make a difference in their own spheres of influence.

In conclusion, Tom Cruise's dedication to mental health awareness, disaster relief, and veterans' rights exemplifies his commitment to championing social issues. Through his advocacy and involvement, he has contributed to raising awareness, supporting affected communities, and advocating for those in need. Cruise's efforts underscore the potential for individuals with influence to effect positive change and inspire others to join the cause.

In the following chapters, we delve deeper into the remarkable career and life of Tom Cruise, exploring his contributions as an actor, his philanthropy, and the enduring impact he has made on the world of entertainment and popular culture. Join us as we celebrate the achievements and reflect on the multifaceted journey of a cultural icon who continues to captivate audiences and leave an indelible mark on society.

Balancing Stardom and Activism: The Challenges and Rewards of Leveraging Fame for Positive Change

For celebrities like Tom Cruise, who have achieved worldwide fame and adoration, there is a unique opportunity to leverage their stardom for positive change through activism and philanthropy. However, navigating the delicate balance between stardom and activism comes with its own set of challenges and rewards. Tom Cruise's journey in this regard provides valuable insights into the complexities of using fame as a platform for positive change.

One of the significant challenges faced by celebrities in leveraging their fame for activism is the scrutiny and criticism that accompanies their actions. Public figures are often subject to heightened scrutiny, with their every move and statement dissected and analyzed. This level of attention can make it challenging for celebrities to navigate sensitive social issues, as any misstep or miscommunication can be amplified and scrutinized by the media and the public. The fear of backlash or negative consequences can be a deterrent for celebrities to engage in activism, as they may fear the potential damage to their career or public image.

Another challenge is striking the right balance between personal beliefs and public responsibility. Celebrities often have strong personal convictions and passions for specific causes, but finding the appropriate ways to champion those causes while respecting diverse perspectives can be a delicate task. It requires careful consideration of how to effectively communicate one's message and engage in meaningful dialogue without alienating or polarizing others. Celebrities must navigate the fine line between expressing their views and respecting the complexity of social issues, while also acknowledging that their influence carries the weight to shape public opinion.

Despite the challenges, leveraging fame for positive change can also yield significant rewards. The first reward is the ability to raise awareness on a global scale. Celebrities possess a platform that can reach millions, providing an opportunity to shed light on pressing social issues that may otherwise go unnoticed. Their visibility and ability to capture public attention can amplify the voices of marginalized communities, spark conversations, and drive meaningful change. The power to mobilize resources and inspire action is a remarkable privilege that comes with fame.

Furthermore, the involvement of celebrities in activism can inspire their fans and followers to get involved in causes they are passionate about. The connection and influence celebrities have with their audience can motivate individuals to donate, volunteer, or take action themselves. Celebrities can serve as role models, inspiring others to use their own platforms and resources to effect positive change. The impact of a celebrity's activism extends beyond their personal efforts, creating a ripple effect that can mobilize a wider movement.

Tom Cruise's own journey in balancing stardom and activism exemplifies both the challenges and rewards. His dedication to various causes, from mental health awareness to disaster relief, demonstrates a genuine commitment to making a positive impact on the world. Despite the controversies and scrutiny he has faced, Cruise's activism has provided him with a sense of purpose and fulfillment beyond his acting career. His influence

and resources have allowed him to
support and champion causes close to
his heart, inspiring others to join the
cause and effect change.

In conclusion, leveraging fame for
activism comes with its own set of
challenges and rewards. Celebrities like
Tom Cruise have the opportunity to
utilize their influence, resources, and
platforms to raise awareness, drive
social change, and inspire others to take
action. Balancing stardom and activism
requires navigating the complexities of
public perception, managing criticism,
and finding the right approach to engage
with social issues. Despite the
challenges, the rewards of using fame
for positive change can be far-reaching,
making a lasting impact on society and
inspiring others to be agents of change.

In the following chapters, we delve
deeper into the remarkable career and
life of Tom Cruise, exploring his

contributions as an actor, his philanthropy, and the enduring impact he has made on the world of entertainment and popular culture. Join us as we celebrate the achievements and reflect on the multifaceted journey of a cultural icon who continues to captivate audiences and leave an indelible mark on society.

CHAPTER SIX

Evolution and Legacy

Adapting to Changing Times: Cruise's Ability to Stay Relevant in an Ever-Evolving Film Industry

In an ever-evolving film industry that constantly demands new talent and fresh ideas, it is a remarkable achievement for an actor to maintain relevance and continue captivating audiences for decades. Tom Cruise's ability to adapt to changing times stands as a testament to his talent, versatility, and unwavering dedication to his craft. Throughout his career, Cruise has demonstrated an exceptional ability to evolve alongside the industry, embracing new challenges, and consistently delivering compelling performances that resonate with audiences.

One of the key factors contributing to Cruise's longevity and relevance is his willingness to explore diverse genres and roles. From action blockbusters to thought-provoking dramas, he has shown a remarkable range as an actor. By embracing a variety of genres, Cruise has continually reinvented himself and expanded his creative horizons. This versatility has allowed him to navigate the ever-changing landscape of the film industry, capturing the attention of audiences across different generations and maintaining a wide appeal.

Cruise's ability to collaborate with visionary directors has also played a crucial role in his ability to stay relevant. Throughout his career, he has worked with acclaimed filmmakers who have pushed boundaries and embraced innovative storytelling techniques. By aligning himself with directors like Steven Spielberg, Paul Thomas

Anderson, and Christopher McQuarrie, Cruise has demonstrated a keen eye for selecting projects that push his artistic boundaries and challenge the status quo. These collaborations have not only resulted in critically acclaimed films but have also ensured that Cruise's performances remain fresh and engaging.

Additionally, Cruise's dedication to authenticity and his commitment to performing daring stunts have contributed to his ongoing relevance. Audiences are captivated by his willingness to push the physical limits, often performing his own stunts in high-octane action sequences. This commitment to realism and the sense of danger he brings to his roles have created an enduring sense of excitement and anticipation among audiences. Cruise's willingness to take risks and push himself physically showcases his adaptability and his understanding of the evolving tastes and expectations of moviegoers.

Furthermore, Cruise has embraced the changing landscape of film distribution and promotion. With the rise of digital platforms and social media, he has utilized these mediums to connect directly with fans, generating excitement and anticipation for his projects. Cruise's active presence on social media platforms like Twitter and Instagram allows him to engage with audiences, share behind-the-scenes content, and generate buzz around his films. By embracing these new channels of communication, he has demonstrated a willingness to adapt to changing times and connect with audiences in new and engaging ways.

It is also worth noting that Cruise's ability to stay relevant extends beyond his on-screen performances. His involvement in the production process, including his roles as a producer and his influence on the creative direction of his projects, has allowed him to shape his career and remain at the forefront of the industry. By actively participating in the decision-making process, Cruise ensures that his films align with the evolving tastes and demands of audiences, further solidifying his relevance and appeal.

In conclusion, Tom Cruise's ability to stay relevant in an ever-evolving film industry is a testament to his talent, versatility, and willingness to adapt. His exploration of diverse genres, collaborations with visionary directors, commitment to authenticity, engagement with changing distribution platforms, and active involvement in the production process have all contributed to his ongoing relevance and enduring popularity. Cruise's ability to evolve alongside the industry while maintaining his unique on-screen charisma has solidified his status as one of Hollywood's most enduring and beloved actors.

In the following chapters, we continue to explore the remarkable career and life of Tom Cruise, focusing on his contributions as an actor, his philanthropy, and the enduring impact he has made on the world of entertainment. Join us as we celebrate the achievements and reflect on the multifaceted journey of a cultural icon who continues to captivate audiences and leave an indelible mark on popular culture.

Impact on the Action Genre: Examining Tom Cruise's Influence on the Portrayal of Action Heroes

Tom Cruise's impact on the action genre is undeniable, as he has redefined and revitalized the portrayal of action heroes in modern cinema. With his magnetic on-screen presence, physicality, and commitment to performing daring stunts, Cruise has left an indelible mark on the genre, influencing the way action heroes are depicted and creating a lasting legacy that continues to resonate with audiences.

One of the key ways in which Cruise has influenced the action genre is through his dedication to performing his own stunts. His willingness to push the boundaries of physicality and put himself in dangerous situations has set a new standard for authenticity and realism in action films. Audiences are captivated by the knowledge that it is Cruise himself performing these breathtaking stunts, adding an extra layer of excitement and credibility to his portrayals. His commitment to practical effects and real-life action sequences has inspired other actors and filmmakers to prioritize realism, resulting in a shift away from excessive reliance on CGI and creating a renewed appreciation for practical stunt work.

Cruise's approach to action roles goes beyond just physicality. He brings depth and complexity to his characters, creating action heroes that are not just one-dimensional but have emotional depth and relatability. Whether it's the conflicted secret agent Ethan Hunt in the "Mission: Impossible" franchise or the determined ex-military officer Jack Reacher, Cruise infuses his characters with a vulnerability and humanity that make them more than just larger-than-life figures. This nuanced approach to character development has contributed to the evolution of action heroes, elevating them from mere archetypes to multidimensional individuals with whom audiences can connect on a deeper level.

Moreover, Cruise's influence extends to the pacing and structure of action films.

His films are known for their relentless energy and pulse-pounding sequences that keep audiences on the edge of their seats. His ability to maintain tension and deliver thrilling set pieces has become a hallmark of the genre. Directors and filmmakers have taken note of Cruise's approach, leading to a shift in the pacing and editing of action films, with an emphasis on dynamic, high-intensity sequences that drive the narrative forward.

Cruise's impact on the action genre can also be seen in the way he has seamlessly blended different genres and storytelling elements. His films often incorporate elements of suspense, mystery, and espionage, creating a hybrid genre that appeals to a wide range of audiences. This blending of genres has allowed action films to transcend their traditional boundaries and attract a broader demographic, appealing to both fans of pure action

and those seeking more nuanced
storytelling.

Furthermore, Cruise's success in the
action genre has opened doors for other
actors, expanding the possibilities for
on-screen heroes. He has demonstrated
that action films can be vehicles for
critical and commercial success,
challenging the notion that they are
solely meant for mindless
entertainment. Cruise's ability to
balance high-octane action with
compelling storytelling has paved the
way for a new wave of action films that
prioritize character development and
narrative depth.

In conclusion, Tom Cruise's influence on
the action genre is profound and
far-reaching. His commitment to
performing daring stunts, his ability to
infuse depth and complexity into his
characters, and his impact on the pacing
and structure of action films have

reshaped the portrayal of action heroes. Cruise's influence extends beyond his own performances, inspiring other actors, directors, and filmmakers to push the boundaries of the genre and redefine audience expectations. His legacy as an action icon is cemented by his enduring popularity and the lasting impact he has made on the way action films are crafted and received.

In the following chapters, we delve deeper into the remarkable career and life of Tom Cruise, exploring his contributions as an actor, his philanthropy, and the enduring impact he has made on the world of entertainment. Join us as we celebrate the achievements and reflect on the multifaceted journey of a cultural icon who continues to captivate audiences and leave an indelible mark on popular culture.

A Lasting Legacy: Assessing Tom Cruise's Enduring Status as a Hollywood Legend and His Contributions to Cinema

Tom Cruise's enduring status as a Hollywood legend is a testament to his remarkable career, undeniable talent, and significant contributions to the world of cinema. Over the course of several decades, Cruise has captivated audiences with his on-screen charisma, versatility, and commitment to delivering compelling performances. His impact on the industry is far-reaching, leaving behind a lasting legacy that continues to shape the landscape of contemporary cinema.

One of the defining factors of Cruise's enduring status as a Hollywood legend is his longevity and consistent success. He has proven to be a bankable star, with numerous box office hits to his name. Cruise's ability to draw audiences to theaters, coupled with his talent and dedication to his craft, has solidified his position as one of the most iconic and recognizable faces in the industry. His enduring popularity is a testament to his ability to connect with viewers and deliver performances that resonate across generations.

Cruise's contributions to cinema extend beyond his box office success. He has worked with some of the industry's most acclaimed directors, including Steven Spielberg, Stanley Kubrick, and Paul Thomas Anderson, showcasing his commitment to collaborating with visionary filmmakers. Through these collaborations, Cruise has pushed boundaries and explored diverse genres, leaving an indelible mark on each project he undertakes. His range as an actor and his willingness to take on challenging roles have earned him critical acclaim and accolades throughout his career.

Furthermore, Cruise's impact on the action genre, as discussed earlier, cannot be overstated. His dedication to performing his own stunts, his ability to blend physicality with emotional depth, and his contribution to the evolution of action heroes have reshaped the genre and inspired a new generation of filmmakers and actors. His influence has been felt both in terms of the technical aspects of action filmmaking and in the way action films are crafted and received by audiences.

Cruise's contributions to cinema also extend beyond his acting prowess. As a producer, he has been involved in the development and production of numerous successful projects, allowing him to shape the creative direction and vision of his films. His production company, Cruise/Wagner Productions, has been responsible for bringing a diverse range of stories to the screen, further expanding his impact on the industry.

Moreover, Cruise's influence as a cultural icon reaches far beyond the realm of cinema. His persona, style, and catchphrases have permeated popular culture, making him a recognizable figure in the global consciousness. From his iconic dance moves in "Risky Business" to his high-flying stunts in the "Mission: Impossible" franchise, Cruise has left an indelible mark on the collective imagination of audiences worldwide.

Cruise's enduring status as a Hollywood legend is also a reflection of his philanthropic efforts and commitment to social causes. His involvement in charitable organizations and his support for causes such as mental health awareness, disaster relief, and veterans' rights showcase his dedication to making a positive impact on the world beyond his acting career. His influence and resources have allowed him to contribute to various initiatives and inspire others to get involved and effect change.

In conclusion, Tom Cruise's enduring status as a Hollywood legend is a result of his extraordinary career, talent, and significant contributions to cinema. His longevity, consistent success, and ability to connect with audiences have solidified his position as one of the industry's most iconic figures. Cruise's impact on the action genre, his collaborations with visionary directors, his influence on popular culture, and his commitment to philanthropy have all contributed to his lasting legacy. As a cultural icon, he continues to inspire and entertain audiences, leaving an indelible mark on the world of cinema.

In the following chapters, we delve deeper into the remarkable career and life of Tom Cruise, exploring his contributions as an actor, his philanthropy, and the enduring impact he has made on the world of entertainment. Join us as we celebrate the achievements and reflect on the multifaceted journey of a cultural icon who continues to captivate audiences and leave an indelible mark on popular culture.

EPILOGUE

The Maverick's Journey Continues

A Glimpse into Tom Cruise's Future Projects and Ambitions

As Tom Cruise's remarkable career continues to evolve, audiences and fans eagerly anticipate his future projects and the new horizons he will explore. Known for his dedication to delivering high-quality performances and his ability to choose diverse and challenging roles, Cruise's future endeavors promise to be exciting and captivating. While specifics regarding his upcoming projects may vary, a glimpse into Cruise's future can provide insight into his ambitions and the directions he may choose to pursue.

First and foremost, Cruise's commitment to the "Mission:

Impossible" franchise remains strong. As the flagship series that has solidified his status as an action icon, Cruise's involvement in the franchise is a testament to his dedication to the character of Ethan Hunt and his passion for thrilling, high-octane storytelling. With several successful installments already under his belt, it is likely that Cruise will continue to push the boundaries of action filmmaking and deliver more exhilarating adventures for audiences to enjoy.

In addition to the "Mission: Impossible" franchise, Cruise has demonstrated a penchant for collaborating with visionary directors and taking on challenging roles. His collaborations with filmmakers such as Christopher McQuarrie, Doug Liman, and Joseph Kosinski have yielded critically acclaimed and commercially successful films. It is reasonable to expect that Cruise will continue seeking out collaborations with talented directors who can challenge him artistically and push the boundaries of storytelling.

Furthermore, Cruise's future projects may also reflect his ongoing interest in exploring different genres. Throughout his career, he has delved into a wide range of film genres, from action and drama to science fiction and comedy. This versatility has allowed him to showcase his talent and adaptability as an actor. As he looks to the future, it is likely that Cruise will continue to embrace diverse roles and venture into new territories, keeping audiences intrigued by his choices and performances.

Cruise's passion for filmmaking extends beyond acting. His involvement as a producer through Cruise/Wagner Productions has given him the opportunity to shape the creative direction of his films and support the work of emerging filmmakers. In the future, he may continue to explore his ambitions as a producer, bringing unique stories and fresh perspectives to the screen. This involvement allows Cruise to contribute to the industry in a broader capacity and nurture new talent.

In terms of ambitions, Cruise has shown a consistent desire to push boundaries and challenge himself. His dedication to performing his own stunts, as well as his commitment to authenticity and realism in his roles, exemplify his ambition to deliver exceptional performances and entertain audiences on a grand scale. This ambition is likely to continue driving him to seek out new challenges, both physically and artistically, as he strives to create memorable and impactful cinematic experiences.

Moreover, Cruise's philanthropic efforts and commitment to social causes indicate a continued interest in making a positive impact beyond the realm of entertainment. His involvement in initiatives related to mental health awareness, disaster relief, and veterans' rights suggests that he will continue to lend his support and resources to worthy causes. It is possible that Cruise will use his influence to champion social issues and inspire others to get involved and effect change.

While the specifics of Cruise's future projects and ambitions may be uncertain, one thing is certain: his dedication to his craft and his desire to entertain and inspire audiences will continue to drive him. As a Hollywood legend, he will undoubtedly leave his mark on the industry through his performances, collaborations, and philanthropic efforts, shaping the future of cinema and leaving a lasting legacy.

Personal Reflections: Insights from Friends, Colleagues, and

Tom Cruise Himself on His Remarkable Career

Tom Cruise's remarkable career in the film industry has left an indelible mark on Hollywood and captivated audiences worldwide. As we delve deeper into his life and achievements, it is insightful to explore personal reflections from friends, colleagues, and Cruise himself, providing a glimpse into the man behind the iconic roles and shedding light on the factors that have contributed to his enduring success.

Colleagues and friends who have worked closely with Cruise over the years have often praised his unwavering commitment to his craft and his relentless work ethic. Many have lauded his professionalism, highlighting his attention to detail and his dedication to delivering the best possible performances. Directors and co-stars have consistently spoken highly of his collaborative spirit, describing him as a team player who brings energy and enthusiasm to the set, fostering a positive working environment. Such reflections underscore Cruise's reputation as not only a talented actor but also a consummate professional.

In interviews and public statements, Cruise himself has often expressed his passion for acting and his love for the film industry. He has shared insights into the joy he finds in the creative process, from studying characters and scripts to the thrill of performing stunts and engaging with audiences. Cruise's genuine enthusiasm for his work is palpable, and his passion shines through in his performances, captivating viewers and leaving a lasting impact.

Cruise's personal reflections also shed light on the mindset and determination that have propelled him throughout his career. He has spoken about the importance of challenging himself and taking risks, both artistically and physically. His willingness to push boundaries and continually seek out new and demanding roles has allowed him to evolve as an actor and maintain his relevance in an ever-changing industry. Cruise's personal reflections offer a glimpse into the inner drive that has fueled his success and continue to inspire both his peers and aspiring actors.

Moreover, Cruise's philanthropic endeavors provide insight into his values and the impact he strives to make beyond the realm of entertainment. His involvement in charitable organizations and causes reflects a genuine desire to use his influence and resources to make a positive difference in the world. Cruise has expressed the importance of giving back and using his platform to raise awareness for issues that are close to his heart. These personal reflections highlight his commitment to social responsibility and his belief in the power of using fame for the greater good.

Additionally, Cruise's reflections on his career and personal growth underscore the lessons he has learned along the way. He has spoken about the importance of perseverance, resilience, and adaptability in navigating the challenges of the industry. Cruise acknowledges that success often comes with setbacks and that it is through perseverance and a willingness to learn from failures that one can continue to grow and evolve. His personal reflections reveal a sense of humility and self-awareness, emphasizing the continuous journey of self-improvement.

In conclusion, personal reflections from friends, colleagues, and Tom Cruise himself provide valuable insights into the factors that have contributed to his remarkable career. His colleagues' praise of his professionalism and work ethic, combined with Cruise's personal reflections on passion, drive, and social responsibility, offer a multifaceted perspective on his success. Cruise's personal insights into his career and personal growth highlight the importance of challenging oneself, embracing opportunities for growth, and staying true to one's values. As we continue to celebrate his achievements, these personal reflections deepen our understanding of the man behind the iconic roles and offer inspiration to aspiring actors and individuals willing to be of impact positively in their chosen fields.

Tom Cruise's Enduring Impact on the Entertainment Industry and His Continued Influence on Aspiring Actors

Tom Cruise's enduring impact on the entertainment industry is a testament to his immense talent, versatility, and dedication to his craft. Over the course of his career, he has left an indelible mark on Hollywood and has become a source of inspiration for aspiring actors around the world. From his iconic performances to his work ethic and commitment to pushing boundaries, Cruise's influence continues to shape the industry and inspire the next generation of talent.

One of the key aspects of Cruise's impact is his ability to consistently deliver compelling and memorable performances. His on-screen charisma, intensity, and emotional depth have captivated audiences for decades. From his breakout role in "Risky Business" to his portrayal of iconic characters like Ethan Hunt in the "Mission: Impossible" franchise, Cruise has demonstrated a remarkable range as an actor. His ability to inhabit diverse roles and bring authenticity to each character has made him a role model for aspiring actors looking to make their mark in the industry.

Cruise's impact also extends to his work ethic and dedication to his craft. He is known for his relentless pursuit of excellence, often going to great lengths to immerse himself in a role. Whether it's spending months training for physically demanding stunts or undergoing extensive research to understand the nuances of a character, Cruise's commitment to his roles sets a high standard for professionalism and dedication. His work ethic serves as an inspiration for aspiring actors, reminding them of the importance of hard work, discipline, and a genuine passion for the craft.

Furthermore, Cruise's influence can be seen in his willingness to take risks and push boundaries. Throughout his career, he has sought out challenging roles and projects that test his abilities as an actor. From collaborating with visionary directors to exploring diverse genres, Cruise's fearlessness and willingness to step outside his comfort zone have set him apart. This adventurous spirit has inspired aspiring actors to embrace new opportunities, push their own boundaries, and constantly seek growth and improvement in their craft.

Cruise's impact on aspiring actors also extends beyond his performances. His philanthropic efforts and dedication to giving back to the community serve as a source of inspiration and remind aspiring actors of the importance of using their platform for positive change. His involvement in charitable causes and his commitment to social issues demonstrate the potential for actors to make a difference in the world beyond their on-screen work. Cruise's philanthropy serves as a reminder to aspiring actors that success should be accompanied by a sense of responsibility and a desire to use their influence to effect positive change.

Moreover, Cruise's enduring popularity and his ability to stay relevant in an ever-changing industry serve as a testament to his adaptability and longevity. Aspiring actors can look to Cruise as a role model for navigating the ups and downs of the industry, evolving with the times, and embracing new challenges. His ability to maintain his status as a Hollywood legend over several decades is a testament to his talent, resilience, and ability to connect with audiences.

In conclusion, Tom Cruise's enduring impact on the entertainment industry and his continued influence on aspiring actors are undeniable. Through his memorable performances, dedication to his craft, willingness to take risks, and commitment to philanthropy, Cruise has become a source of inspiration for aspiring actors around the world. His ability to captivate audiences and his status as a Hollywood icon serve as a reminder of the power of talent, hard work, and perseverance. As the industry continues to evolve, Cruise's influence will undoubtedly continue to shape and inspire aspiring actors who strive to make their mark in the world of entertainment.

Printed in Great Britain
by Amazon

25515295R00073